FOR
Bronwyn and Daphne;
Isabel, Sam, and Oliver;
Blue and Beau;
and Max — with lots
and lots of love
N. D.

FOR
Mick, with love
B. G.

Text copyright © 2011 by Nicola Davies
Illustrations copyright © 2011 by Brita Granström

First U.S. edition 2012

Library of Congress
Cataloging-in-Publication Data is available.
Library of Congress Catalog Card Number pending

ISBN 978-0-7636-5548-8

12 13 14 15 16 17 SCP 10 9 8 7 6 5 4 3 2 1

Printed in Humen, Dongguan, China

This book was typeset in Ice Age D.
The illustrations were done in acrylic.

Candlewick Press
99 Dover Street
Somerville, Massachusetts 02144

visit us at www.candlewick.com

CANDLEWICK PRESS

Dolphin Baby!

NICOLA DAVIES

illustrated by BRITA GRANSTRÖM

Tail first, head last,
Dolphin POPS out
into the blue.

He's creased and crinkled
from being curled inside his
mother. His tail flukes are
floppy from being folded for
so long. He's all brand-new,
but right away, he swims
up . . . up . . .

Baby dolphins are born one at
a time and are called calves.

6

up ...

7

Ppppfffff!

His blowhole opens when it touches the air,
and he takes his first breath.

Mom is right beside him, and they
breathe together in perfect time.

Ppppffff!   Ppppfffff!

Dolphins are mammals
like you and me, so
although they live
all their lives in the
sea, they must come to
the surface to breathe air.

When Mom swims, Dolphin knows that
he must follow. Swimming and following
are things baby dolphins are
born knowing . . .

but suckling
takes a little
practice.

Newborn dolphins suckle two
or three times every hour,
for just a few seconds
each time.

Dolphin dives
beneath his
mother to find
one of her nipples;
they are tucked into slits
under her belly. It takes
him a while to get it
right, and then he needs
to take another breath
or two.

Dolphins communicate
with lots of different
whistles.

12

Mom and Dolphin rest together.
Dolphin rubs his tummy on Mom's
round head. Mom strokes him
with her flipper. She whistles to him
a whistle that is just hers—
her name in dolphin-sound:

Shreeee-eep!

He whistles back—but for now
his whistles make no sense . . .
they're just baby talk!

Every dolphin has one whistle that's its own,
a bit like our human names.

Others have arrived to take
a look at newborn Dolphin.
They're all around.
Their voices fill the water.
They're curious about
this new member
of their group.

14

But Mom knows that what
new babies need is peace
and quiet. Soon she
swims away, with
Dolphin close
beside her.

Dolphins are very sociable and live in close groups of around fifteen, which split up and re-form all the time.

In just a few weeks, Dolphin has grown so much! His folds and creases are all gone; he's smooth and gray. He doesn't swim beside Mom now, the way newborn babies do, but underneath her tail like **bigger** calves.

16

Male calves make best friends with one or two other males that they'll know all their lives.

Now he's old enough to make friends.
The youngsters play—
chasing . . . carrying . . . showing off . . .

but then Mom whistles,
and Dolphin knows he must go back.

Playing can't take
all day. Mom
needs to swim off
and hunt for food.
Dolphin stays close,
but sometimes . . .

Adult dolphins spend
about a third of
every day hunting
and eating.

Mom ZOOMS after fish,

too fast for him to follow . . .

or

dives

deep,

where

he

can't

go.

It takes several
years for calves
to be able to dive as
deep as adults can.

Dolphin hears her C L I C K I N G,
using sounds and echoes to find food
where it's too dark or deep for her to see.

He clicks, too, and listens to the echoes of his
voice so he can hear Mom's shape and movement
when she's out of sight.

A dolphin's round forehead is called a melon.
It helps the dolphin make clicks and find
its way around using sound.

Mom doesn't stay away for long.
She whistles— *Shreeee-eep!* —
when she's coming back. She brings
a fish for Dolphin—still alive.

He C L I C K S at it
to learn the echo-shape it makes
so that one day he'll be able to catch his own.

Then Mom eats it up in two quick bites.
No need to share, as Dolphin is
still fed by her milk.

Dolphins sometimes work together to herd fish but often hunt alone.
They never share a fish that they catch, not even with their calves.

It's been SIX months since Dolphin popped into the blue. He's not a grown-up yet, but he's not a baby anymore, either . . .

because today

Dolphin has caught his first fish!

Snacking on fish near the surface is just one of many ways dolphins learn to catch their dinner.

And when Mom
whistles her
sound-name—
Shreeee-eep!—
he doesn't whistle
back in baby talk,
but answers
with a whistle
that's his very own—

This whistle will be
his for all his life.

His name in Dolphin.

Dolphin calves stay with their mothers for about four years. They start to have babies at about age twelve and can live for twenty to thirty years in the wild.

TAKING CARE OF DOLPHINS

There are more than thirty different kinds of dolphins in the world, including dusky dolphins, white-sided dolphins, spinner dolphins, spotted dolphins, and striped dolphins. The ones in this book are bottlenose dolphins, which are found in almost every ocean except the very coldest ones.

I've been lucky enough to see them in lots of different places, from chilly gray seas to warm tropical ones, and wherever they are, bottlenose dolphins are always ready to play. They jump out of the water, do somersaults and back

flips, and bow ride at the front of boats. Watching them is a delight.

Right now, there are still plenty of bottlenose dolphins in the world's oceans, but they are threatened by the risk of being caught in fishing nets, by pollution, and by overfishing, which takes away their food. We need to take better care so that our seas will stay full of dolphins and dolphin babies for centuries to come.

N. D.